BASKETI
LEGENDS

Mark Woods

D0526362

CLASH
by ticktock

Copyright © ticktock Entertainment Ltd 2009

First published in Great Britain in 2009 by ticktock Media Ltd,
The Old Sawmill, 103 Goods Station Road, Tunbridge Wells, Kent, TN1 2DP

project editor and picture researcher: Ruth Owen
ticktock project designer: Simon Fenn

Thank you to Lorraine Petersen and the members of nasen

ISBN 978 1 84696 943 0 pbk

Printed in China

A CIP catalogue record for this book is available from the British Library.

No part of this publication may be reproduced, copied, stored in a retrieval system or transmitted in any form or
by any means electronic, mechanical, photocopying, recording or otherwise without prior written permission of
the copyright owner.

Picture credits (t=top; b=bottom; c=centre; l=left; r=right):
AFP/Getty Images: 10, 11, 20, 25r, 29. Getty Images: 25l, 31. CINIGLIO LORENZO/CORBIS SYGMA: 16. Dr. James
Naismith Basketball Foundation, Almonte, Ontario, Canada: 6. NBAE/Getty Images: 4-5, 8, 9, 13, 15, 18, 19, 21, 22,
23, 24, 26-27, 28. Shutterstock: OFC, 1, 6 (background), 7, 10-11 (background), 13 (background), 18-19 (background),
30-31 (background). Sipa Press/Rex Features: 5. Sports Illustrated/Getty Images: 2-3, 12, 17.

Every effort has been made to trace copyright holders, and we apologise in advance for any omissions. We would be pleased
to insert the appropriate acknowledgments in any subsequent edition of this publication.

CONTENTS

TIP-OFF

Basketball is one of the most popular and exciting sports in the world.

You can slam dunk it.

You can shoot a three-pointer.

You can make the perfect pass to a team-mate.

Vince Carter slam dunks!

It's the only place where stealing is a good thing.

China's Yao Ming at the 2008 Beijing Olympics.

And you don't have to be tall to play...

...but it helps.

HOW IT STARTED

Basketball was invented in the USA in 1891. It was invented by a Canadian sports teacher named Dr. James Naismith.

Naismith wanted to find an indoor game that his football team could play in the winter to keep fit.

Dr. James Naismith

The game was played with baskets that were used for carrying peaches. Each team had nine players.

There was no shot clock, so players took a long time to shoot. The first game ended 1-0.

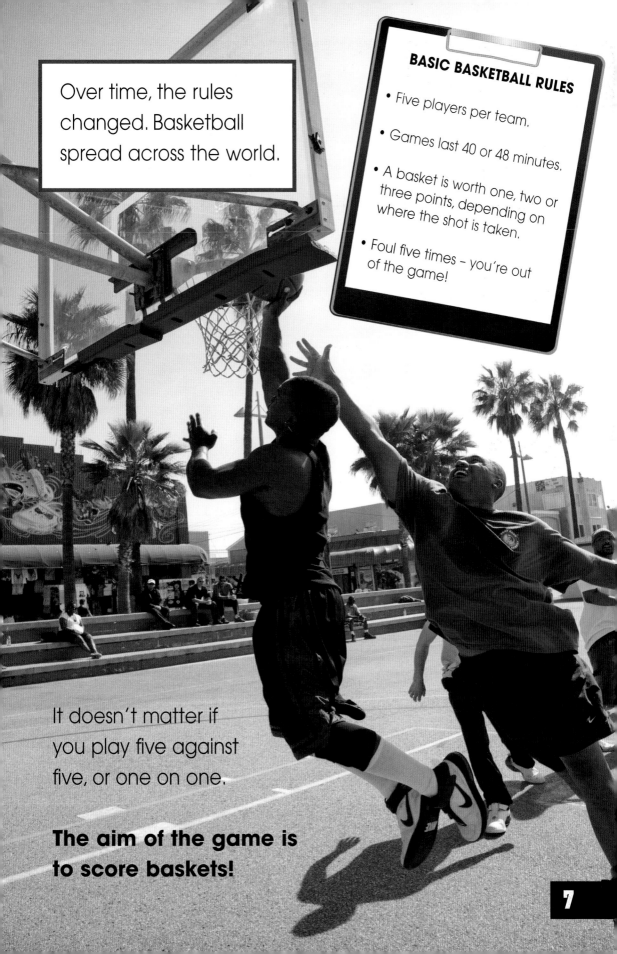

Over time, the rules changed. Basketball spread across the world.

BASIC BASKETBALL RULES

- Five players per team.
- Games last 40 or 48 minutes.
- A basket is worth one, two or three points, depending on where the shot is taken.
- Foul five times – you're out of the game!

It doesn't matter if you play five against five, or one on one.

The aim of the game is to score baskets!

THE NBA

The National Basketball Association (NBA) is the most famous league in the world.

The NBA has 29 teams in the USA and one in Canada.

The Boston Celtics win the 2008 NBA Championship.

Each team plays 82 games in the regular season.

The best 16 sides qualify for the play-offs.

The team that wins the play-offs is the NBA champion.

The WNBA (Women's National Basketball Association) league began in 1997. It is made up of 14 teams in the USA.

The women's game is less physical than men's basketball. There is more passing and shooting than dunking.

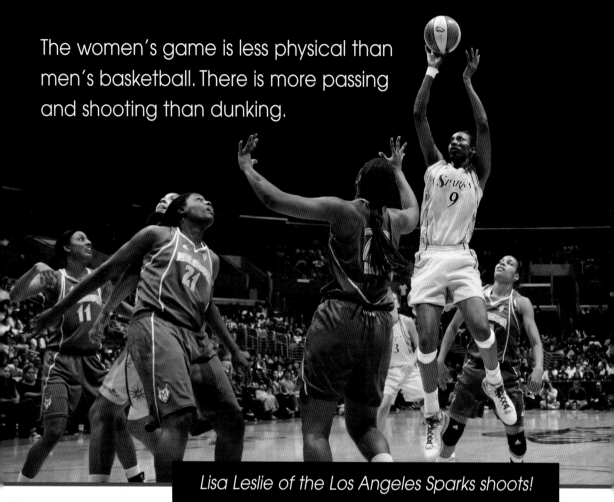

Lisa Leslie of the Los Angeles Sparks shoots!

" In boys, it's ingrained in their heads that to dunk is just the highlight of basketball. For girls, shooting technique, making baskets and free throws is taught more. "

Lisa Leslie

In Europe, the best teams play in the Euroleague.

The most successful teams are CSKA Moscow, Maccabi Tel Aviv, Barcelona and Panathinaikos.

The strongest competitions are in Spain in the ACB League, and in Greece.

The British League is called the BBL (British Basketball League).

Maccabi Tel Aviv (in yellow) and CSKA Moscow in the 2008 Euroleague final.

INTERNATIONAL CHAMPIONSHIP WINNERS

- 2008 Olympics – USA
- 2007 European Championships – Russia
- 2007 Asia Championships – Iran
- 2006 World Championships – Spain

International teams compete in championships, and in the Olympic Games.

The USA has won 13 of the 17 Olympic men's tournaments. The USA has also won six of the nine women's events.

2008 Olympic final

Pau Gasol, Spain

Jason Kidd, USA

MICHAEL JORDAN

Michael Jordan is probably the best basketball player in history.

He played for the Chicago Bulls for 13 seasons and won six NBA titles.

Michael Jordan

Jordan's nickname was "Air Jordan". He could jump so high, it looked like he was flying through the air!

Jordan was also an excellent defender. Lots of fans only get excited when players get baskets. But it is important to stop the other side from scoring to be successful.

Jordan was named the "Most Valuable Player of the NBA" five times. This award is given to the best player of the season. He retired in 2003.

RIVALS

Every sport has rivals!

Rivals are two teams or two players who really want to beat each other every time they meet.

One of the biggest rivalries in basketball is between the Boston Celtics and the Los Angeles Lakers.

Magic Johnson of the Lakers and Larry Bird of the Celtics were huge rivals in the 1980s.

> " The first thing I would do every morning was look at the box scores to see what Magic did. I didn't care about anything else. "
>
> *Larry Bird*

NBA TITLES
- Magic Johnson 5
- Larry Bird 3

Larry Bird

Magic Johnson

GLOBETROTTERS

The Harlem Globetrotters are a special team who mix up awesome basketball skills with making crowds laugh!

The Globetrotters were formed in 1926. They have visited over 120 countries.

In the early 1970s, the Globetrotters had their own cartoon series on TV. They have also appeared in lots of movies.

From 1971 to 1995, the Globetrotters won 8,829 games in a row. They have won over 22,500 games!

*1978 – Meadowlark Lemon shows
off his ball spinning skills in Paris, France.*

KOBE AND SHAQ

Kobe Bryant turned professional when he was 18 years old. He was the youngest NBA player ever.

In 2006, Bryant scored an incredible 81 points in a game between the Los Angeles Lakers and the Toronto Raptors.

Kobe Bryant shoots a free throw for his 81st point.

Bryant won three NBA championships with the Los Angeles Lakers in 2000, 2001 and 2002.

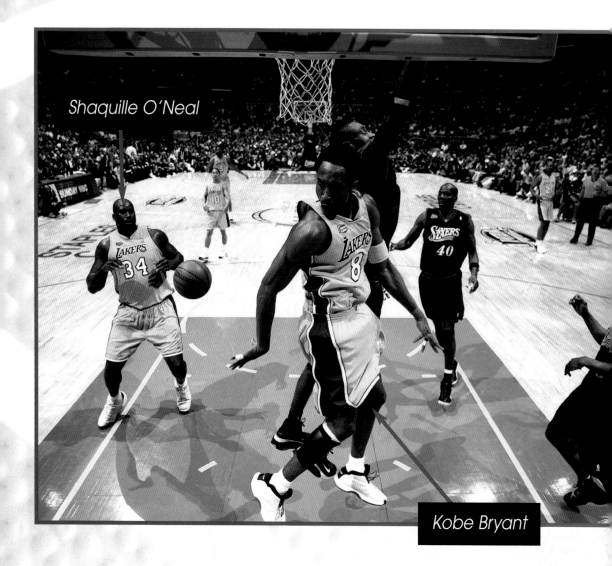

Shaquille O'Neal

Kobe Bryant

Bryant's team-mate for those championships was 2.16-metre-tall Shaquille O'Neal.

"Shaq" is a busy guy. He's made movies, rap music and he is a police officer!

WORKING TOGETHER

**When two players play well together,
they are very difficult to stop.**

Dirk Nowitzki and Steve Nash were team-mates
at the Dallas Mavericks. They always knew
where the other one was on the floor.

Steve Nash

Dirk Nowitzki

Nowitzki was the
first European to
be named "Most
Valuable Player of
the NBA", in 2007.

Nash was the first
Canadian to get
the award, in 2005.
He also got the
award in 2006.

The job of the point guard is to run the team and help his team-mates.

Utah Jazz point guard John Stockton had 15,806 assists. That's more than any player in the NBA.

John Stockton

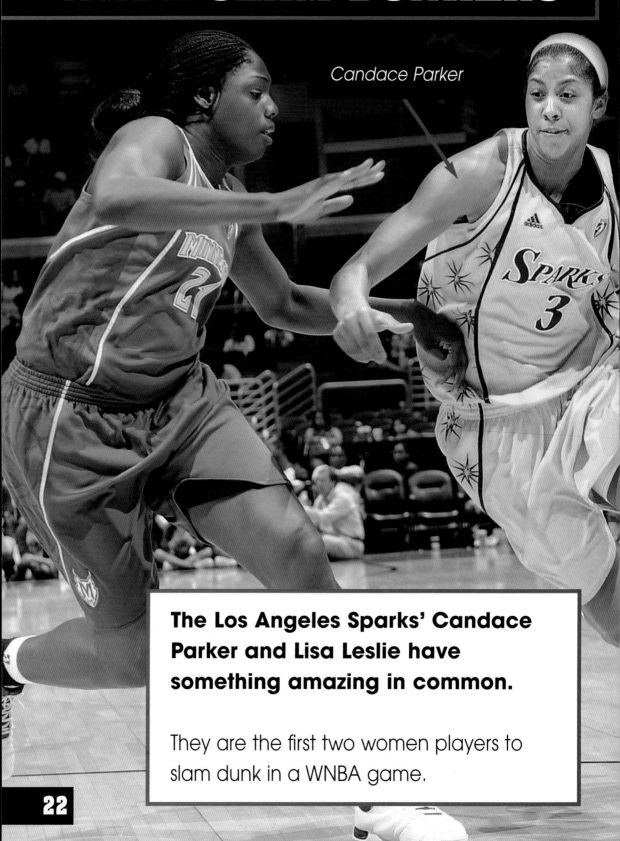

WNBA SLAM DUNKERS

Candace Parker

The Los Angeles Sparks' Candace Parker and Lisa Leslie have something amazing in common.

They are the first two women players to slam dunk in a WNBA game.

Lisa Leslie

Slam dunk!

Lisa Leslie has won four Olympic gold medals, two WNBA titles and three "Most Valuable Player" awards.

BASKETBALL GIANTS

Yao Ming from China is one of the most famous players in the world.

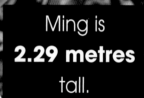

Ming is **2.29 metres** tall.

Ming is a centre for the Houston Rockets.

Each year, fans get to vote on who will play in the NBA's All Star game. In 2005, Ming received 2,558,278 votes – that's a record!

The tallest ever NBA player is Gheorghe Muresan from Romania.

Muresan is an awesome **2.31 metres** tall. ←

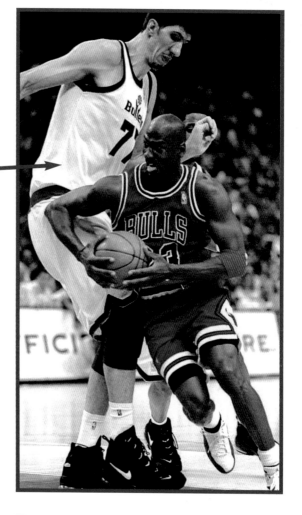

The smallest NBA player ever is Muggsy Bogues. He is **1.6 metres** tall.

" I always believed in myself. That's the attitude I took out on the floor – knowing that I belonged. That with my talents, my abilities, there's a place for me out there. "

Muggsy Bogues

LUOL DENG

Luol Deng is a British player. He plays for the NBA's Chicago Bulls and the UK national team.

" Basketball is something that I really love. It's something that I could play all day. I never really get bored with basketball. "

Luol Deng

In his first NBA season, Deng was named on the NBA's All-Rookie Squad.

Many fans say he's the best British NBA player ever.

Luol Deng

Superheroes

Dwight Howard plays for the Orlando Magic.

He's a powerful jumper. This allows him to do spectacular dunks!

Howard dresses as Superman to win the 2008 Dunk Contest.

2008 – LeBron James in action against Spain at the Beijing Olympics.

LeBron James plays for the Cleveland Cavaliers. He led them to the NBA finals in 2007.

James is able to play as a guard, forward and centre.

At high school in Ohio, James grabbed 2,657 points, 892 rebounds and 523 assists.

Need to know words

All-Rookie squad A team of the best five rookies.

assist A pass that leads to a score.

centre Usually the tallest defender in the team.

defender A player whose job is to stop the other team scoring.

forward A strong player who plays close to the basket.

foul Called by the referee if the rules are broken.

free throw A shot worth one point after a foul is called.

guard A player who defends furthest from the basket.

ingrained Something (such as a belief or habit) that is strongly implanted in someone's mind.

league A group of teams who compete to win a championship. Each team plays all the others in the league at least once.

physical Playing close to your opponent with lots of energy.

play-offs The end of season competition.

point guard The player whose job it is to bring the ball from one end of the court to the other.

professional A player who is paid to play.

rebound Grabbing the ball after a shot is missed.

rookie A player's first year in the league.

season The period of time during which a league plays for a championship.

shot clock A clock which shows the 24 seconds that a player has to take a shot.

slam dunk Jumping really high above the rim of the net and throwing the ball down through the hoop.

stealing Taking the ball away from an opponent.

three-pointer A shot from long range which is worth three points.

ALL-TIME GREATS

- The most famous US Olympic team was the 1992 "Dream Team". It featured Michael Jordan, Magic Johnson, Larry Bird, John Stockton and Karl Malone. In one game, they beat Angola by 68 points!

- The all-time points record currently goes to Wilt Chamberlain of the Philadelphia Warriors. In 1962, he fired 100 points against the New York Knicks.

The 1992 "Dream Team" receive their Olympic gold medals.

BASKETBALL ONLINE

Websites

http://www.nba.com

http://www.fiba.com

http://www.euroleague.net

http://www.basketball247.co.uk

Index